Dear Lord, I Desire To Be Whole

Women Healed of Life Experiences

Study Book

Catrina D. Garrett

Foreword

I am very proud to say Catrina Garrett is my wife. I am in awe of the gift God has placed in this mighty woman of God. She is an inspiration and motivator. She is always willing to share and help others, leading them to the potential God has place in them. As her husband, I have watched her to overcome many battles she's faced in this life, seeking the Lord with all her heart to be made whole. As you read this study book you will discover she is dedicated to see many women to be free, to live at peace, and to be made whole!

—Apostle Tommy Garrett
Thy Kingdom Come Global Ministries

Acknowledgements

This Book is dedicated to my Lord and Savior Jesus Christ for making me whole from experiences in my life. To my Beloved and devoted Husband Apostle Tommy Garrett who has walked by my side through the good and the bad. My best friend and soulmate, I love you so much. To my Parents Carol and Berry Perkins who have made me into the woman I am. To my children Eric, DeAndre, Christopher, Durrell, and Terell who have given me the reason to stay focused in my commitment to serve as a child of God. To my sisters Melinda and Niki thank you for always believing in me. To my Best friend Evangelist Latasha Jones I am so grateful for all you have done. The late nights we spent in editing and the girl talk about our Jesus. Thank you so much! To Ramonda Moore-Brown thank you for all of the encouraging words and motivation you have shown me. To Apostle Michael and Teresa Levy for always showing us love. To our friend Ben Bowers, thank you for all your support. To Pastors Bill and Donna Pfeffer and the Tabernacle family thank you so much for all your support and love. To Apostle Earthy Gaskin and the JMI family words can't express the dedication and the support you all have shown me. To all the Apostles and Prophets who prophesied this book thank you for letting God use you to use me.

Introduction

My Journey To Wholeness

As a child, I was growing up as your average kid with dreams of being much more than I really was. I was raised as a military child and my family never really went to church. Not having many friends as I grew up caused me to feel isolated and I began to substitute boyfriends as a way to escape the feeling of rejection. As a result of these choices, I became pregnant at age seventeen, failed to complete high school and had two abortions by the time I was twenty-three years old. Later, I married and had four children, but I was divorced by the age of twenty-seven years old. I lived a life of hopelessness in countless relationships trying to fill the void of feeling unloved and unwanted. I suffered from severe depression spending days and nights laying in my room hiding in the dark of the shadows of my pain, I felt like a failure to the point of trying to take my own life. I was a single mother with four children and no job. All I could think of was who is going to love me for me.

In 1999, I was at a point in my life when I became ready for change. I was tired of the club scenes and the dating games. The truth of the matter, I was ready to be whole. I met my wonderful husband Tommy when I first moved to Florida in 1989, but it wasn't until 1999 when we ran into each other again at a local night club. At the time, I was reluctant about getting into a serious relationship with Tommy. He talked about getting back in relationship with God, and of course, at that time was something that I did not want to hear. If you had mentioned anything about commitment to Christ, it would have steered me away.

Over the course of time, Tommy and I began to develop a close relationship. Periodically he would witness to me about Jesus which encouraged me to tell him about the dreams I had of Jesus coming back. Tommy told me that it was the voice of God calling me. I was thinking to myself there is no way God is call me with all of the terrible things I have done in my life. But it was in the year of 2002 at the age of thirty-two years old when I felt the Lord drawing me; in April of 2002, I gave my life to the Lord. Tommy and I were married in December. I was so excited to experience my new life and to start a new beginning.

Within a year of our marriage, we began to experience the trials of life that caused me to slip back into depression. I was so overwhelmed with the issues in my life. My oldest son was sent to prison, my second oldest son had children out of wedlock, my youngest son was failing in school, and we started having financial problems. It seemed as if my life was crumbling all around the same time. My husband and I were called to the ministry and I thought things would be better, but it grew worse. As we experienced church hurt and rejection from fellow co-laborers in ministry, I became withdrawn to myself and I shut down. This affected my marriage, my job, and my family. Reflecting my failures, I blamed myself for the disappointments in my life. I concentrated on being a perfectionist in everything I would put my hands to, which brought on more stress and pain.

My husband and I argued every day; I blamed him for every mistake or problem we faced. I constantly nagged at him to be a Godly man because I worried about how people thought of us. Trying to perfect or make my husband into the man of God I wanted him to be caused more damaged than good. My poor children would get Bible verses thrown at them day after day. I did not realize this was turning me into a monster and causing pain for my family.

One day, I had enough. I got down on my face and cried out to the Lord all of my issues. I did this in a selfish way because I still blamed everyone else. The Lord revealed to me that I was the issue. As a woman of God, I allowed my issues in life to beat me down trying to fix it myself or to hide them in the shadows. When He showed me myself, I said to him "Lord I am dying." He spoke to my inner man and said "That's the purpose, you need to die to your flesh and really let me in so you can walk in my Spirit". It was like a touch from heaven. My spiritual eyes opened and I saw a glimpse of a spiritual battle between the Spirit of God and satan over my soul. After confessing Jesus Christ, satan continued his manipulation in control of my life. He wanted to make a liar out of me. When I came to myself, I realized I was dying to live. At that moment, the Lord made me whole. It gave me a new perspective on life. I began to let go of everything of the past to use as a testimony of my deliverance to wholeness.

Our lives take on journey and along this path we run into obstacles that challenge our faith. The purpose for this is because God is the author and finisher of our faith. We are born into this world having many issues, but if we allow the Lord to clean us up and make us whole we will see blessings that will flow as a testimony to others. I am a testimony that you may be healed of every issue you face in this journey. If you are willing to let Jesus in, I can assure you He can fix it.

The woman with the issue of blood most likely felt as if she was dying, but she had enough faith to reach out and touch the savior. What is so amazing is this woman might have been dying in the physical, but she did not let her issue kill her spirit. She still had a little faith in her spirit that caused her to speak to the issue for her freedom. Like many of us, we have no control of the issues in our lives, but we have access to a savior who completely knows our situation. God doesn't require us to have unshakable, unwavering, mountain moving kind of faith, in order to work miracles in our lives. Sometimes just like the woman with the issue of blood all we need to do is have enough faith to just barely touch the hem of Christ's garment. If we can do that, then He can use His miraculous power on our behalf. Journey with me through this manual to experience wholeness in Jesus Christ.

Contents

Lesson 1

A Woman's Desire To Be Whole

Through this study let's first learn the story of the woman with the issue of Blood.

SCRIPTURE REFERENCE:

Mark 5:25-34

†*And a certain woman, which had an issue of blood twelve years, And suffered many things of many physicians, and spent all she had, and was nothing bettered, but rather grew worse, When she heard of Jesus, came in the press behind, and touched his garment. For she said, "If I may touch but his clothes, I shall be whole. And straightway the fountain of her blood was dried up". And she felt in her body that she was healed of the plague. And Jesus, immediately knowing himself that virtue had gone out of him, turned him about in the press and said, "Who touched my clothes"? And his disciples said unto him, "Thou seest the multitude thronging thee, and sayest thou, Who touched me"? And he look round about to see her that had done this thing. But the woman fearing and trembling, knowing what was done in her, came and fell down before him, and told him all the truth. And he said unto her "Daughter, thy faith has made thee whole; go in peace, and be whole of thy plague".*

CONFRONTING THE ISSUE

A desperate and lonely woman banned from human contact who had been ill for twelve years pushed her way from isolation to receive her healing. Not only that, but she told the truth; she told him about her issues.

A. Ask yourself how many times in your life when faced with issues are you immediately isolated?_____

_____

B. What caused you to feel isolated?_____

_____
_____
_____

According to the law of Moses, she was unclean (Leviticus 15:19, 25)

†*And if a woman have an issue, and her issue in her flesh be blood she shall be put apart seven days: and whosoever toucheth her shall be unclean until the evening. 25 And if a woman have a issue of her blood many days out of her time of her separation, or if it run beyond the time of her separation; all the days of the issue of her uncleanness shall be as the days of her separation she shall be unclean.*

- Her Husband could not touch her
- She could not enter the place of worship
- Whatever she touched became unclean

Like this Woman in our scripture lesson, we all have experienced in our lives sickness, broken hearts in relationships, delay in goals, and lost of loved ones. No one has the perfect life; however, we do have the perfect sacrifice (Jesus Christ) that can make us whole if we reach out in faith.

Separation can cause extreme worry, fear, sleep depravity, stress, and anxiety. I can completely understand how this woman felt, yearning for freedom giving everything she had to physicians to get her breakthrough. This woman didn't just want to be healed she desired to be whole.

She heard of this Jesus performing miracles and like this woman with an issue we need to see the vision beyond the tears. She saw her healing. She believed. She stretched her faith! —

Romans 10:17
†*So the faith cometh by hearing, and hearing by the word of God*

A. How have some experiences in you life affected your everyday living?

_____

_____

_____

_____

_____

B. How do you feel about yourself at this point in your life?

_____

_____

_____

C. Are you willing to open up? _____

_____

_____

Lesson 2

Living In The Shade Of Darkness

LIVING IN THE SHADE OF FEAR

The woman with the issue of blood, lived in the shadows for twelve years. Her condition caused extreme body weakness and weight loss. She was not just affected physically but mentally as well. It must have taken every moment of effort just for her to get out of bed on a daily basis, day after day, and year after year living in complete defeat.

Often times in our lives, we are faced with issues that no one understands. In my life, being rejected caused me to live in the shadows for years. Someone could say something so small and immediately I shut down in isolation. I didn't want to talk about it I just cried myself to sleep. It affected my relationship with Jesus and everyone around me. I wanted to shut everyone and everything out of my life.

You can be in the shadow of your pain, but you must realize wholeness takes time. The Apostle wrote to the Corinthian Church not to lose heart—

2 Corinthians 4:16-17

†*For which cause we faint not; but though our outward man perish, yet the inward man is renewed day by day. For our light affliction, which is but for a moment, worketh for us a far more exceeding and eternal weight of glory;*

One of the enemies greatest tactics is to use fear to keep us hiding in the shadows.

A. Fear of admitting what are we afraid of

B. Fear of what others think of us

C. Fear of coming out of our comfort zone

A woman who has been abused or broken can tend to live in shadows due to the fear of reoccurrences or the feeling of isolation. We can use things or addictions to substances (sex, drugs, alcohol, hoarding, and etc.) as a substitute to hide our pain and emotions.

God knows we will struggle with anxiety. He knows insecurities within would press constantly in our thought process drawing us away from him into fear. That is why over and over in the bible we hear, "fear not be of good courage"! In this world we live in we will have trouble Jesus stated in—

John 16:33

†*These thing I have spoken unto you, that in me ye might have peace. In the world ye shall have tribulation: but be of good cheer; I have overcome the world.*

A. Are you living in fear of acceptance?_____

_____

_____

_____

_____

B. In what way are you using your shadow to cover your securities?_____

_____

_____

_____

_____

_____

In life it is easier to live in the shadows especially when we are hurting. You may have experience a separation in marriage, unresolved family circumstances, frustration due a failed to business or career, or lost of a loved one. When my ex-husband and I separated, the fear of rejection caused me to live in the shadows. I hid myself from new commitments due to fear of acceptance. I was constantly in and out of relationships. These experiences in life can leave open chapters in our hearts so the enemy can substitute it with guilt, fear, and shame to rob us of experiencing abundant living.

John 10:10
†The thief cometh not, but for to steal, and to kill, and to destroy: I am come that they might have life, and they might have it more abundantly.

Notice how Jesus phrases the word **might** which tells us that we must make an effort to desire to be whole. Satan desires to keep you in a shadow boxed in from your Identity, self-esteem, or destiny. Don't believe the lies of the enemy. You are able to be whole. You must declare it over yourself. The woman with the issue of blood did this very thing. She did like David, encouraged herself in Jesus.

Samuel 30:6
†And David was greatly distressed; for the people spake of stoning him because the soul of the people was grieved, everyman for his sons and for his daughters: but David encouraged himself in his God.

OVERCOMING FEAR

Fear can shadow our sense of the world as we know it. Fear causes us to remember negative events which reinforce our sense to hide in the shadows. We can use numerous ways to hide. For instance, we can withdraw ourselves from socializing in our church, losing enthusiasm in our worship, disconnecting from our families, or becoming unethical in work.

I believe that the woman with the issue of blood used that very moment of overcoming her fear to receive her healing; she pressed through the crowds. Many times we need the reassurance from people in the decisions we make in our lives. When we are called to do a work for the kingdom of God, it is natural for us to seek man's approval rather than God's mandate due to fear of failure and acceptance. I believe we should press through and seek to reach toward our destiny.

We as women called to do a work in the ministry can face many challenges that can lead us to fear. It is vital for us to trust in the word of God to lead us into the steps ordained by the Lord. This does not mean in the process we are not going to experience issues, but we can be made whole as we continue in the working process. We should not be anxious, which will only lead to worry and fear, but to seek the Lord's direction through our prayer life.

Philippians 6:1

Be careful for nothing, but in everything by prayer and supplication with thanksgiving let your request be made known unto God.

Are you ready to overcome?

Write down the fears your are ready to overcome:_____

_____

_____

_____

_____

_____

_____

_____

_____

_____

_____

_____

God's Ultimate Purpose

GOD'S DIVINE WILL & PERMISSIVE WILL

God's divine will cause many obstacles in life. We are challenged to the purpose and the plan for our lives. He has a divine will and He has a permissive will. His divine will is sovereign and pre-destined to be used for His purpose.

Jeremiah 29:11
For I know the thoughts that I think toward you, saith the Lord, thoughts of peace, and not of evil, to give you an expected end.

The permissive will of God is what He permits. A note point is that the fact He permits something does not mean it is His will. Like the woman with the issue of blood God permitted her to seek after physicians to heal her from her issues, but His divine will was to make her whole. She must have heard or saw the miracles of Jesus which cause her to take a leap of faith to believe. She must have thought I may not understand my situation, but I am going to trust in Jesus to heal me.

A. Do you know what your purpose is in your life? Write it down_____

_____
_____
_____
_____
_____
_____
_____
_____
_____
_____
_____

Often when we are broken we limit our perspective our purpose of our being, we may ask ourselves "why am I here"? or "why am I going through this"! I declare to you take the limits off. God has a plan for your life, let go of your fears and trust Him. Let your faith conquer over your silence. We all have had some misfortunes in our lives. Don't dwell on them, reflect on the blessings and focus toward the outcome.

Sometimes our disobedience to God or being out of the will of God; will permit some things to happen. Just like when Abraham and Sarah received the promise of having a son for God's purpose, they chose a handmaiden because they did have patience for the true promise.

• Genesis 15:4

†And he brought him forth abroad, and said, Look now toward heaven, and tell the stars, if thou be able to number them: and he said unto him, So shall thy seed be.

•   Genesis 16:2

†Now Sarai, Abram's wife, had borne him no children. She had a female Egyptian servant whose name was Hagar. And Sarai said to Abram, "Behold now, the Lord has prevented me from bearing Children. Go in to my servant; it may be that I shall obtain children by her". And Abram listened to the voice of Sarai.

How many times have we heard the voice of God to inspire us into what He had purposed us to do and we take it upon ourselves to complete the mission according to our own way. Or perhaps you received a promise from God, but it did not come the way you expected, so you decide to help God, but in the midst to make it a total disaster.

The bottom line God does not need our assistance to complete our purpose. He needs our trust and obedience. When we started our ministry, I did not want to hold our services at this particular hotel conference room we are presently at now. I remember when my husband said "This is where God wants us to be". I was so angry I tried to steer my husband in another direction, but my husband was firm in what God spoke.

We went through a lot of disappointments, but I learned to trust the Lord. In result of my trust, God opened up so many doors for us. In addition, He gave us favor to use the conference room for free. What if I would have continued to discourage my husband from the purpose God had for us to do because of my disbelief? I realized this was a part of my process to becoming whole. God told us to step out in faith with no money and no one to help us to start the ministry.

Write down some of the poor choices you have made because of distrust:

_____

_____

_____

_____

_____

GOD'S PURPOSE

• God created us to worship Him * You were planned of God's Pleasure

Ecclesiastes 12:13

†*Let us hear the conclusion of the whole matter: Fear God, and keep his commandments: for this is the whole duty of man.*

• God delights in our fellowship * You were formed for a family

James 1:18

†*Of His own will begat He us with the word of truth, that we should be kind of firstfruits of his creatures.*

• We are His disciples * You were created for a mission

Matthew 28:19-20

†*Go ye therefore, and teach all nations, baptizing them in the name of the Father and of the Son, and of the Holy Ghost. Teaching them to observe all things whatsoever I have commanded you: and, lo, I am with you always, even unto the end of the world. Amen.*

GOD'S PURPOSE VS SATAN'S PURPOSE

Satan's purpose is to use the issues in your life to bind you in chains of discontentment, and to prevent you from living in peace and fellowship with others and to complete your purpose.

• To Kill * Kill your worship for God

2 Corinthians 2:11

†*Lest Satan should get and advantage of us: for we are not ignorant of his devices.*

• To steal * Take your joy and isolate you from the family of believers

Ephesians 4:15-16

†*But speaking truth in love, may grow up into him in all things, which is the head, even Christ: from whom the whole body fitly joined together and compacted by that which every joint supplieth, according to the effectual working in the measure of every part, maketh increase of the body unto the edifying of itself in love.*

• To Destroy * Destory your spirit, forfeiting you to bring others to Christ {The mission}

1 Peter 5:8

†*Be sober, be vigilant; because your adversary the devil, as a roaring lion, walketh about, seeking whom he may devour:*

When God has a plan for you life, you will not be able to have the full understanding of His purpose. I can totally attest to this when I heard the voice of the Lord calling me into ministry. I felt like "Why me, God with all the issues I have in my life and your calling me"? But like the woman with the issue of blood she rested in the assurance that "God is who He is"! Does that mean she wasn't afraid when she reached out? It is only when we completely trust God that He can give us the power of His direction for His ultimate purpose!

Can you trust in your purpose driven by God? Write how:

_____

_____

_____

_____

_____

_____

_____

_____

_____

_____

_____

_____

_____

_____

_____

_____

_____

_____

My Prayer for you:

"I pray that from His glorious, unlimited resources He will empower you with inner strength through His Spirit. That Christ will make His home in your hearts as you trust in Him. I pray for your roots to grow down deep into Christ's love and keep you strong my sister. And that you may have the power to understand the will of God for your life. I pray that the source of His hope will fill you completely with joy and peace because you trust Him. Then you will rise and overflow with confident hope through the power of the Holy Spirit that you are purposed and you are not mistake because you are fearfully and wonderfully made".

WHAT IT MEANS TO BE WHOLE

Wholeness is a deep commitment to God more constant awareness of the indwelling (Holy Spirit) Christ.

James 1:17

†*For the law was given by Moses, but grace and truth came by Jesus Christ*

The Greek word for whole is sozo (The lexicon gives this definition) — To rescue from danger; to save, to keep safe and sound. Now there is a passage of scripture in the Bible that tells us that through Christ we can have a sound mind.

2 Timothy 1:7

†*For God hath not given us spirit of fear, but of power, and of love, and of a sound mind.*

There are some things over which you have no control, and to dwell on them serves no useful purpose. Adopting the "poor me" attitude gives no promise and offer no gain. The one thing I found in being whole is when I learned to commit to God and serve the need for others, I felt complete.

A. Have something or someone has cause your commitment to God to be unfaithful?

_____

_____

_____

WHEN GOD BREAKS US

You may be in a point in you life, "Why me" syndrome. When we think of wholeness, we automatically think the of matter of sickness, disease, injury, or material wealth. Wholeness however, is a matter of harmony in your mind body and soul. For instance, like the story of the man who was born blind in the Bible. God used his illness to manifest His Glory.

John 9:2

†*And his disciples ask him saying, Master, who did sin, this man, or his parents, that he was born blind? Jesus answered, "Neither hath this man sinned, nor his parents: but the works of God should be made manifest in him".*

Throughout life, we are confronted with many issues on a every day basis. The purpose for the breaking is for the making. When God breaks us, He does so with the purpose of putting us back together again. .

WALKING STEP BY STEP

You might be in a season of feeling like "There's no way out"! or "God where are you"? God has not forgotten you, in fact He will reveal His plan and purpose to you step by step. Very rarely does He give insight into the total plan He has for you, but you must learn to trust Him.

Job 13:15

†*Though He slay me, yet will I trust in Him: but I will maintain mine own ways before Him.*

It may very well seem as if you are wasting away daily, but if you will look beneath the surface to the inner work God is doing in your life. That is look from a spiritual perspective vs carnal thinking.

I remember one day I was driving home from work receiving a devastating call from my son's public defender; he was going to face a ten to fifteen year sentence for a crime he did not commit, but because he had so many previous charges they were pinning the case against my son. At that time I could not afford an attorney; after hanging up the phone with him I was ready to give up I felt like I was going to have a anxiety attack. Suddenly, I heard the Holy Spirit said to pull over and pray! I prayed "Father in the name of Jesus! You said you can turn the heart of a king any which way you wish." "Send everything you got in heaven in that courtroom on behalf of my son"!

The next day at church someone got up and stated "The Lord told me someone's child is facing some time in prison for a charge they did not commit"! Your prayer's have been answered your son will not do the time suggested by the state's attorney's request". At that moment I tore that church up jumping and screaming with joy. On the court date, God worked a miracle on my son's behalf and turned the case around. His sentence was reduced to thirty six months.

In the midst of my son facing this prison sentence, God used this incident to break me and to make me whole at the same time. I had to look at what I was experiencing with my son from a spiritual perspective vs carnal thinking. I must admit it was very difficult, but when I fully put my trust in the Lord, it worked on our behalf. The fiery trials of life are meant to perfect us for the purpose of God.

James 1:2

†*My brethren count if all joy when ye fall into divers temptations; knowing this that the trying of your faith worketh Patience.*

Our God is a miracle working God, but He can't perform the miracle without us being apart.— Apostle Catrina Garrett

18

For the Lord to bring us to wholeness, He must deal with the areas in our lives that keep us from wholeness. My issues were lack of trust, pride, anger, fear, and bitterness. The trouble many of us have is that we don't see the spiritual principles involved in the various situations and circumstances we encounter on a daily basis. Even though we have been born again in our spirits we habitually live by carnal thinking.

Romans 8:6

†*For to be carnally minded is death; but to be spiritually minded is if life and peace.*

God desires for us to totally depend upon him in every issue we face in our lives. When we began to see it the way God sees it, this is the first step to wholeness. We are able to overcome our emotions but motivated through the spirit to be confident in knowing the outcome of our issues.

In spite of the circumstance our hope is in Christ. If we can trust Him through the trials of life, we can be made whole from sickness, emotional losses, and failures.

A. In what perspective are you viewing your current situation?

Write it down_____

_____

_____

_____

_____

_____

_____

_____

_____

_____

_____

_____

_____

_____

_____

_____

_____

We Are What We Speak

WORDS THAT GIVE LIFE OR DEATH

Just like we use the term we are what we eat. We are what we speak.

Life and death are in the Power of the tongue —

Proverbs 18:21

†*Death and life are in the power of the tongue: and they that love it shall eat the fruit thereof.*

You will discover the way we use our tongue has power. It can be a tree of life or a weapon of mass destruction. The woman with the issue of blood in desperation did not only reach out, but spoke to herself "If I may just touch the hem of garment, then I will be made whole". Because she spoke life to her issue, thus she received her healing.

The old saying "sticks and stones may break my bones, but words can never hurt me" is a lie and a deception. Many women have suffered issues for years and some unto their death because of hurtful words. A woman can die spiritually because of something someone said. Also, a woman can live because of something someone said. The Bible vividly describes bitter words as arrows—

Psalms 64:3

†*Who whet their tongue like a sword, and bend their bows to shoot their arrows, even bitter words.*

WHAT FILLS YOUR HEART

Jesus said in Luke 6:45 "out of the abundance of the heart the mouth speaks". You might have suffered from others tearing you down from the words they spoke. This could have occurred when you were a child through your young adult life, or even right now. As women, we are so vulnerable to words good or bad. But you must understand, this is a part of your process to wholeness. You can't control others from speaking death over your situation, but you can certainly speak life over your circumstances.

No matter how your situation in your life looks to you now, I declare that you speak Life! The more you declare the word of God over yourself, you will start to feel healing to your broken-heart. You will begin to let go of all bitterness and resentment. Then you will make every effort to be at peace in your mind, body, and soul. You will desire be to kind and compassionate to others and out of your belly will flow rivers of living water.

John 7:38

†He that believeth on Me, as the scripture hath said, out of his belly shall flow rivers of living water.

Describe what you may fill in your heart at this moment:

_____

_____

_____

_____

_____

_____

_____

_____

_____

_____

_____

_____

When we are hurt by the words spoken over us, God uses this as an instrument to make us whole. When must learn not to let it take root in our hearts, that is what the word of God is for. It helps us to speak wholesome words over our lives. I was in a season in my life when my heart was in critical condition, especially when we started in ministry because of so much rejection. It was building up layer upon layer. I spoke so much death because my heart was so heavy in the pain I felt. I was like a heart attack waiting to happen. Every time I spoke death my husband would immediately speak life.

I was a wounded soldier on the battlefield who could not help anyone until I was made whole. It wasn't until the Lord revealed to me that He was hearing the words I spoke and I was accountable for the words spoken. That's when I realized I am what I speak and I will have what I speak also.

Matthew 12:36

†But I say to you, That every idle word that men shall speak, they shall give and account thereof in the day of judgment.

I learned to practice speaking words of life instead of words of destruction. I noticed that when I did not focus my the current situation and put my trust in the word of God, His promises changed my perspective.

Use the shattered pieces in your life as a lamp for Christ to shine through.

— Apostle Catrina Garrett

REVERSE THE CURSE

You have the power to reverse the negative words spoken over your current situation to bring forth life. How many times did you ask God why did He allow people to say hurtful things? Well, that's a good question because I have asked Him too. I believe He allows it because this is how He can receive the glory out of our lives.

Often times in your life it may seem as if you are not able to move forward because of hurtful words. As the old saying goes— "Hurting people, hurts people". Keep in mind this is the building process of your faith in God. In order to be made whole you have to experience some brokenness. I have found it is easy to love people when they are pleasant and kind to me, but when they are evil or mean that's when I am in need of God's word to help me to love and forgive them.

Matthew 5:44

†*But I say unto you, Love your enemies, bless them that curse you, do good to them that hate you, and pray for them which despitefully use you, and persecute you;*

In other words you hold the power if you apply the words Jesus spoke in your heart to speak peace to your spirit this builds character to your spirit. Remember others are watching and you are to show them "yes I am going through, but the God I serve is making me in the process"! In every assignment we face, as women to build the Kingdom of God, we need to be careful in what we say and how we say it.

Especially leading women in the ministry, whether you are a preacher, or a Pastors wife. We definitely have to be made whole to stand with vision and with our husbands to be able to speak the promises of God concerning the His purpose. Because we hold a valuable position and we have to endure a lot of responsibilities, it is a necessity that we practice speaking the principles of the word of over ourselves, our husbands and our ministries. In times past, I have seen wounded women who was in leadership destroy churches. As I said earlier that same spirit tried to rest upon me until I reach out to touch the savior for my inner healing.

Write down a positive word concerning you:

_____

_____

_____

_____

_____

Lesson 6

Take Action

CHALLENGED TO TAKE DOMINION

The woman with the issue of blood took dominion over feeling defeated. She was to the point of desperation to see her breakthrough. Let's face reality, worldly counsel cannot bring complete wholeness; it only leads to temporary results which keep us in the shadows. The unbelieving world knows nothing about the divine spiritual life. I am not saying as far as a physical health condition we should just stay home and pray, but when you have been to every doctor with no results the only option is to seek the Lord in prayer.

Psalm 147:3
†He heals the brokenhearted and binds up their wounds [curing their pains and their sorrows].

When we are challenged with emotional distress worldly counsel can lead us into more destruction. For example, you're dealing with depression you see a counselor or a doctor they pop a pill in your mouth then send you on your way still with the same issues. I can attest to this because I have been there at a point in my life. It wasn't until I received Jesus through salvation as the working of Holy Spirit brought freedom and wholeness to my mind, body, and soul.

The worlds system can only provide us with a temporary fix. We must recognize openly that the most valuable facet of our being truly the eternal facet of our lives is being strengthened, nourished, and refined through Jesus. That is the dimension of wholeness that truly counts.

Key note*

No matter how long we struggle, our time of trail is only momentary. Even if we have affliction or time of brokenness that last for years. Even decades God is working in our behalf. What is that compared to all eternity?

2 Corinthians 4:16-17

†For which cause we faint not; but though our outward man is perish, yet the inward man is renewed day by day. For our light affliction, which is but for a moment, worketh for us a far more exceeding and eternal weight of Glory;

Nothing can compare for what awaits us, but in the process to becoming whole it will be worth it all.

—Apostle Catrina Garrett

23

The number one key factor to taking action to becoming whole is Faith in God. We need to build our faith in God's love. We do this by meditating and reading the word of God daily, but also confessing that He loves us. Surround yourself with Godly believers and **stay active** in a local Church. I have seen this happen countless times when a woman is seeking to be free in Christ from abuse, drugs, alcohol, depression, suicide, or sickness, she was not able to remain to stay whole, due to lack of communication with the Pastor or the members. Before long her attendance decreases and she falls right back to where she was healed from. In spite of every attack I faced from the moment I confessed Jesus into my heart, I did not let anything separate me from Him. I might have severed some relationships with people and I even separated myself also, but I stayed determined in my relationship with Jesus.

Are you ready to take action to becoming whole?

_____
_____
_____
_____
_____
_____
_____
_____

Stay focused in the healing process as I said earlier "Speak Life"! As we do this it will build determination in the process of wholeness. Set the goals you would like to accomplish in building the Kingdom God. But most of all become a servant, as you begin to serve others you will see your true identity and purpose. This fills every void in your life because as you are serving the needs for others, it is serving your purpose.

Take action to fix our eyes on the unseen. If it looks bad at anytime we are broken and we start to loose heart, we must submit our lives to God. Satan uses distractions to get us off focused in what God is doing in us. God is making us whole, beginning in the unseen spiritual dimension of our lives. Basically He is putting things back in there proper order; the spirit first, the soul second, the physical third. He making us Whole again!

In the book of Jeremiah, God told him "Before I formed you in the womb I knew you". In other words God knew all the issues we would face long before we experienced them. Like the woman is the issue of blood, **God see's us through the crowds.** If we can just hold on, and embrace the process we can be made whole.

In the shadows of my darkest hour I am secure the Lord is my

shade, because He covers me, my light can shine through. —

Apostle Catrina Garrett
Priceless Women Ministries

Often we perceive in life that it is "all about me". We hear mottos like: "I have to do what it takes to make me happy" and "I have got to get mine". While I am sure we have all felt this way one time or another; we must not adapt this feeling as a lifestyle. Because truth-be-told, we are all going to need somebody at some time in our lives. Unfortunately, we will experience adverse circumstances as a buffer to mold and shape us into whom we are intended to be. Thus, it is all about us. It is "all about us" portraying more Christ like characteristics such as: love, joy peace, longsuffering, kindness, goodness, faithfulness, gentleness, and self-control. And the more we do this, people will see our good work, however, GOD will get all the glory! Our flesh has to be crucified so that others might live.

When life is topsy- turvy and seems misconstrued; rest assured, GOD hasn't made a mistake! It is HIS tests in revealing to us where we are slack in our walk with Him. He loves us too much to let us remain in our sinful state. We must take a pledge and make a stand to give GOD our lives. HE gives it a whole new meaning. So yes, it is all about us being delivered from the slightest bit of frustrations and compulsive complaining. We must examine ourselves daily and inquire GODLY wisdom to make the necessary corrections in order to live victoriously. Yes, life can be unpleasant at times, but trouble doesn't last always. It is up to us to make up in our minds to choose the life which our Father has abundantly prepared for those who love and obey Him. Thou life can be difficult; we can conquer its obstacles by consistently applying GOD's principles.

Good News.....JESUS has promised to never leave us nor forsake us. If we acknowledge and call on Him, He will answer us and show us great and mysterious things. HE will shed light on those areas in our lives which needs surrendering. It's imperative that we are diligent in taking care of all that GOD has individually instructed for us to do. And subsequently, He will take care of all the other things which concern our lives. If there is anything that is praise worthy, it is that we are becoming more and more Christ-like; essentially that is what we are *all about*!

"*Timeless Treasures*" with Evangelist Latasha Jones

facebook www.facebook.com/latasha.jones

The Prayer Of Salvation

Father God, I thank you for who You are and all that You are. I humbly submit my life to You. I confess with my mouth that Jesus Christ the Lord, and I believe in my heart that You have raised Jesus from the dead. {Romans 10:9} I believe that Jesus is now seated with You in Heavenly places and will intercede on my behalf {Ephesians 1:20 & Romans 8:43} Please forgive me of all of my sins and cleanse me of all unrighteousness.

I thank you Lord that I am now a new creature in Christ Jesus. {2Corinthians 5:17} Thank you for creating in me a clean heart and renewing a right spirit within me. I Thank you that I am now Your child and as such am entitled to all of the blessings and benefits that accompany salvation. {Psalms 103}

Thank You my Lord, for healing, wholeness, and restoration in every area in my life

In Jesus Mighty Name—

AMEN

Connect with Apostle Catrina Garrett on:

www.facebook.com/apostlecatrina.garrett or Catrina Garrett

www.instagram/kingdomgirl1

Like our page

www.facebook.com/page/Thy-kingdom-come-Global-Ministries-Inc-Revelation-2217
www.facebook/pages/The-Prophetic-Zone